She Graduated Early: from Earth to Glory

Betty Jessie Maddox

Copyright © 2017 Betty Jessie Maddox

All rights reserved. No part(s) of this book may be reproduced, distributed or transmitted in any form, or by any means, or stored in a database or retrieval systems without prior expressed written permission of the author of this book.

ISBN: 978-1-5356-1092-6

Preface

God created you and said, "That's good!" YOU are soo special to God, who created you and made you to be an AWESOME being. He gave you your own set of fingerprints and made you an individual, unlike any other. He gave you talents and a skill set to be developed to an amazing level, so that you could be a blessing to mankind and ALL of His creation. It is His desire that you surmount life's challenges, which HE HAS EMPOWERED YOU TO OVERCOME THROUGH FAITH IN HIM. But God did not say that ALL of life would be easy. He did say that He would be there for us all during those times when trouble challenges our way. This is the story of a young lady who believed that and would not "settle" for less than she thought God would help her to overcome. Meet Tazanya deAnn Maddox, whose story I hope will be an encouragement to you. She would say, "Go forward, trusting God to make your way straight, to empower you to overcome, and honor your faith in Him, to be there whispering into your ears that you can do it, through Jesus Christ, in whom you have placed all trust." BE BLESSED! BE AN OVERCOMER! BE AN INSPIRATION TO OTHERS!

Contents

Preface iii
Chapter 1: Born to Be an Example 1
Chapter 2: A Major Bump in the Road 7
Chapter 3: God Steps In/Tee Steps Up 11
Chapter 4: New Heights to Reach/A God to
    Glorify 17
Chapter 5: A Major Blessing on the Way 23
Chapter 6: God's Grace Magnified! 27
Chapter 7: Graduation to Heaven 33
Chapter 8: Blessed Assurance 39
Awards/Recognitions/Achievements (through Christ
    who strengthened her) 47
In gratitude for prayers, love, care, support, and friendship through it all 49

Chapter 1

BORN TO BE AN EXAMPLE

"I CAN DO ALL THINGS **through Christ, who strengthens me" (Phil. 4:13).** That's what she believed. **SO CAN YOU!**

She was scheduled to graduate in less than a month from C. L. Harper High School but she graduated early, from earth to Glory, exchanging her cap and gown for her heavenly robe and crown!!!

Family and friends call her "Tee." Her full name is Tazanya deAnn Maddox. "Favored Grace" is what her first name means, and I know that being given that name was a prophetic choice, not of my choosing, but of God's. God gave me her name ten years before she was born, and it was longer than that before I knew its meaning, even though I'd tried to discover it. Later, it just "dropped" into my lap. (We were told to expect our first child, who, as it happened, would be a handsome boy, Eric.) For some reason, I continued to keep that name in my heart, even after seven years later, when our second son, Kirk, another handsome little boy, was born. Just in the nick of time, God sent Tee, whose spirit was that of the 60s, as she loved old-school music and possessed old-school values. She was special right from the start—well-behaved, a little shy at first knowing, an excellent student who loved school, had a winning personality, and possessed admirable character. So, did you say, she sounds PERFECT? Well, since none of us is perfect, I'll just say that she came close. Soon, though, we were to learn that that does not keep challenges from your doorstep or your body, but her faith in God kept her strong and guided her way.

We watched Tee grow, and develop lofty plans for a life FULL of accomplishments spanning many decades ahead. Tee tested into the Gifted Program as she began pre-school and continued to follow that educational track through high school, taking Honors classes and later Advanced Placement classes, where she continued to perform well. She was a student who did her homework, even with a creative flare where allowed, shared other gifts and talents as a cheerleader from her elementary school years throughout high school, sang in her church choirs from the children to the youth, performed in musicals in middle school, sang inspirational music on special programs and in talent shows, and even performed on the amateur stage at the Sweet Auburn Festival as she and her dad palled around one Saturday. She had hopes of one day singing the National Anthem at a Braves' baseball game. Tee participated in fairs, and in her high school years, became a forensics/communicative competitor through debate, oratory and interpretation events. Because of her concern for our financial challenges, with two brothers in college at the same time for a year, she said, "Mama, you and Dee Dee (their name for Aubrey, their father) won't have to worry about sending me to college because I'm going to become valedictorian and receive a full scholarship to school." TWO goals she was determined to achieve. These became her goals just before her medical challenge began to take shape; her white blood cells began to develop their rogue status—unknown to her or us. BUT THAT DID NOT STOP HER! SHE PRESSED ON DAILY!

It was interesting watching her grow and develop her own unique personality, work her way through the slight speech impediment that became obvious with certain words as she sang, watching her create a strange vocabulary, calling fat pork meat "rubber meat" and the sheets on the bed the "cold covers." It was also humorous watching her call Dee Dee when her brothers, especially

Kirk, "messed with" her, only to tease him when Dee Dee made him stop. She loved herself some David Justice, which may have fueled her hopes of singing the National Anthem at a Braves' game. One of our friends, who worked with the Braves organization, heard of her crush on David and was instrumental in her receiving a special ball autographed just for her, just before her homegoing. Michael Jackson and the Jackson 5, the Temptations, Boyz II Men, and the Five Heartbeats, from the movie by the same name, were her male music idol crushes. Whitney Houston, Stephanie Mills, and Boyz II Men were the singers whose music she sang. And she was very colorblind because she also loved Lou Diamond Phillips, especially in his *La Bamba* movie role, Johnny Depp from the *Jump Street* TV series, and let's not forget the New Kids on the Block. She also loved Morris Brown College where Kirk was enrolled, and where both Aubrey and I had attended. Every time we'd go to a game there, she'd be right in tow—loved, loved, loved the Marching Wolverines Band. She also loved, loved, loved shopping anytime possible, and she was quite the trendy dresser.

Remember that she was near perfect, but not there yet, so there were those few times when disciplinary measures were in order, but we soon found that sending Tee to her room without TV did not work well, as she'd get a book, climb in bed, and enjoy reading, or get her tape recorder and sing along with Whitney, Stephanie, or Boyz II Men, or better still, tape herself singing along with their soundtracks. Boy were we glad that the times of punishments were few, because we'd run out of ideas that worked.

As she grew, during the elementary years, she outgrew many girls her age in height and felt a little awkward about it at times. So Mama to the rescue, we enrolled her in a Model, Inc. course as a middle school young lady. Their graduation culminated with a fashion show. It was awesome, and she had the opportunity to take one of her "strolls" down the runway to Michael Jackson's "Bad."

Chapter 2

A Major Bump in the Road

At this point, life for her and us took a challenging turn. The older Tee became, the more she became concerned about her girlish figure, and that concern could become the signpost to us of the challenges ahead as we all decided to lose a few pounds, some more than others. We began to watch what we ate and tried a manageable diet. As we all exercised our bragging rights one Saturday morning, Tee felt a small lump on the side of her stomach, which we decided was perhaps a fatty tumor; however, we decided that we should be sure what was happening. So off to the doctor she and I went, stopping by the mall first, then on to the doctor.

After an examination, her doctor, too, thought as we did but decided that we needed to be sure. So off again we went for X-rays. Following the exam, the technician, too, was puzzled, as he'd not seen anything about which to be concerned, and as he asked further questions of us (Why did your doctor send you for X-rays? Where is the lump? etc.), he decided to X-ray Tee's chest. The good and the bad happened in that moment. He did see something of concern, and so we went--back to the doctor, who decided to confirm with additional X-rays at Egleston Children's Hospital. By now my heart was pounding, wondering what it could be. Egleston confirmed that something was going on. What? They were not yet sure of the diagnosis but did know that Tee (and I) would not be returning home that day. And this was the news that I had to break to her, and later to her father, who was awaiting our return. Now "We 5" (family nickname) were all anxious to know. Needless to say, the news did not go over well with her, but she was anxious to get it all cleared up, hoping to return home soon. It took two to three days for them to be sure. As they quizzed her and me and did further tests, marking the spot, since the lump had disappeared, so that other doctors could easily find it as they came in to examine her. We became somewhat numb, yet still not expecting what they finally determined. They diagnosed Tee with leukemia, and then, when explained, the water began to flow, especially from her. We tried to be strong parents, in hope that it would keep her from becoming overly frightened by this news. And so the real journey began. The funniest thing that happened was that, once the diagnosis was made, that lump disappeared and could not be felt again, as if it were there just to guide them and then leave. HOW AWESOME our GOD IS!!!

Treatment was determined, with a stay in the hospital to be followed by a long stay at home, the trips to the doctor and the side effects to be expected. We met some AMAZING people while she was hospitalized: Mrs. Sydney, who always brightened her day with things from stuffed animals to other trinket-like items; C. J., who could always find her veins quickly (boy, was that appreciated!); Nan and Sally, whose personalities were so cheerful, always inspiring hope; and Dr. Alvarado, her primary doctor during hospital stays, one whom she knew would do all that he could to restore her health. ALL were her favorites, and we grew to love them as extended family. We were really concerned that she understand that she'd lose her hair, as she was now stepping into her teen years when young ladies love their hair. She'd just started really going to the beautician. How would she take the real understanding? She worried about school and her grades but homebound schooling was done, and her teacher for much of this time, Mrs. Bessie Monroe did a great job in keeping her up with her classes. Her classmates were saddened and sent her messages, etc. often. As the days crept on, so slowly, our deflated balloon would again begin to fill up with air, making our efforts to see the lemonade that would come from these sour lemons more visible. Rev. Henderson, Rev. Thomas, and Rev. Matthews, Pastoral Care Minister visited and encouraged her/us often. Many members of our church prayed regularly for her well-being. Her faith and her will also fed ours, and we remembered that it was We 5 (plus so many others in our family and our friends), our faith in God, and our belief that "This, too, shall pass."

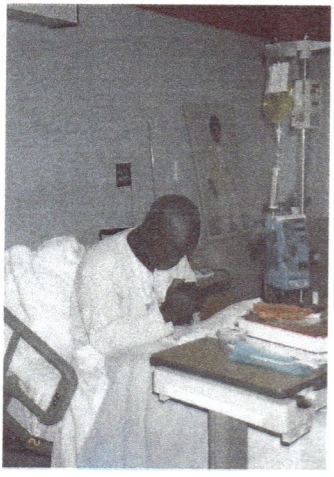

Chapter 3

God Steps In/Tee Steps Up

So many amazing things began to happen!!! Before all of this happened, Tee had asked if she could go to the high school where I taught, but I was a firm believer in supporting neighborhood schools and had told her she'd attend the same school her brothers did; however, now it made sense that she attend my school, so that on doctor-visit days, we both could get to school as soon as possible, and so that I could monitor her feeling throughout the day when necessary. But almost no days was there a need to be concerned, as she felt well most days at school. After each visit, too, she was anxious to get to school, not wanting to miss much. **Just before this all began as well**, her Dad who had worked the assembly line at Ford Motor Co. for over twenty years, received a promotion to Quality Control, which meant that he'd now work in an office, and, unlike before, would now be able to take her to the doctor some days and bring her to school. **Heaven-sent orchestration!!! He who knows all was looking out for her/our good BEFORE THIS ALL BEGAN.**

But the challenges would still come. This young eighth grader, who'd just begun to think about her hair as young girls do, marched into our room one day with razor in hand and announced, "Dee Dee, go ahead and shave it off!!" With this, she flashed a determined smile that had to have masked some emotional pain but made us soooo proud of her. When finished, she rubbed her bare head and marched back into her room.

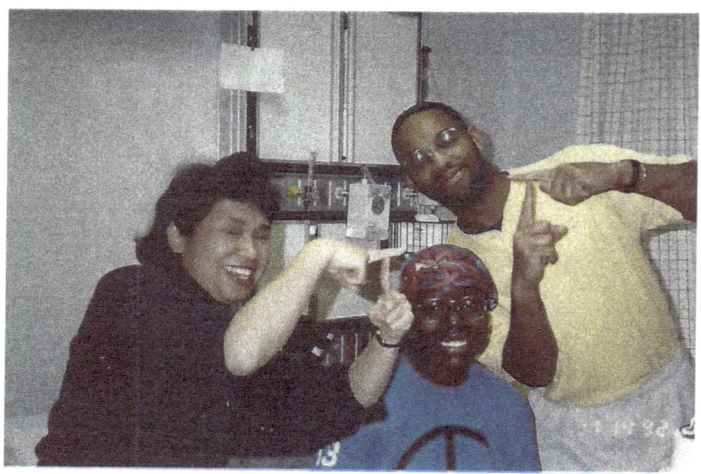

She and her Dad went by the wig shop one day following her doctor's appointment, and he purchased her the wig of her choice. It suited her well, but at several junctures, we tried to convince her how amazing she looked without it, as her hair was now beginning to return. But she was not concerned about herself. She was concerned about how it might make her peers feel seeing her bare head and knowing the history behind it all. Near perfect, I told you. But there were times when, just as she'd exit wherever she'd been and was on her way home, she'd throw the wig off, rub her head, and smile at its liberation. Remember though that she was a shopaholic and a stylish young lady, so, of course, she had to have at least two or three different wigs, varying in length and style, as she did lose her hair twice, and she'd

have to start anew with each occurrence. Between those times, though, as her hair grew back to within an inch or two, she'd discard the wig and sport her own hair in a cute cut. Her Grandmother (my Mom) and her Aunt Ann, my sister-in-love, were a major help to us, and she just loved their company when she had to remain home for a few days after some extended and other precautious hospital stays. That allowed us both to go to work. They were a major BLESSING to all of us. The boys enjoyed having them around as well.

Just before all of this adventure began, Tee'd auditioned for a major part in the musical *Purlie* and had been chosen to play Missy. She was to return to school at the end of April/first of May. The production would be in mid-May, but her teacher would not allow them to cast anyone in her place, expecting her to return well enough, prepared enough to perform. AND SO SHE WAS, AND SO SHE DID!!!!!!!!! She learned her part and the music they were to sing within a two- or three-week period. And since, by then, everyone knew of her medical challenge, it was such a testament to her GOD'S FAITHFULNESS, AND HER FAITH IN GOD TO

WHOM ALL PRAISES WERE GIVEN, FOR WHOM SHE DID PERFORM—AND DID SHE PERFORM WELL!!! She continued to stand on her faith through those months and through the years that would stretch ahead of her.

Chapter 4

NEW HEIGHTS TO REACH/A GOD TO GLORIFY

NOW OFF TO HIGH SCHOOL!!!!!!!!!!!!!! Tee met many new friends and shared her challenges with some of them. They, and others who soon discovered for themselves, were amazing and quite supportive. A very few, who realized that she wore a wig and didn't understand why, were insensitive, and a little inhumane at times, but others championed her plight and chastised those who in later years would apologize for such behavior. All who met her were inspired by her on some level, and she was very respectful and loving to all whom she met.

She continued her rigorous course of studies, became a cheerleader, debater, and anointed inspirational singer at banquets, funerals, assembly programs at school, and with her church choir. Three of her favorite songs were sooo prophetic as you will see if you read the lyrics to "One Moment in Time," "The Greatest Love of All," and

Stephanie Mills' "Home". They spoke to her life's journey. As I write, I'm even more convinced that just as each of us is uniquely made with special talents, gifts, and abilities, God desires that ALL of us experience our moment(s) in time, our time(s) to give to and receive from others placed around us to BLESS and be BLESSED. She sang "Happy Birthday" to a fellow student who cried as other students said that they wanted her to sing to them on their birthdays. She even sang the Temptations' "Silent Night" one year with the C. L. Henderson Male Chorus (with which her Dad and brothers sang). She also sang on the Ford Motor Company Talent Show (in which her father also participated), a talent show at our church, Ben Hill United Methodist Church, and a duet with me at our UMW's Mother-Daughter Banquet. On

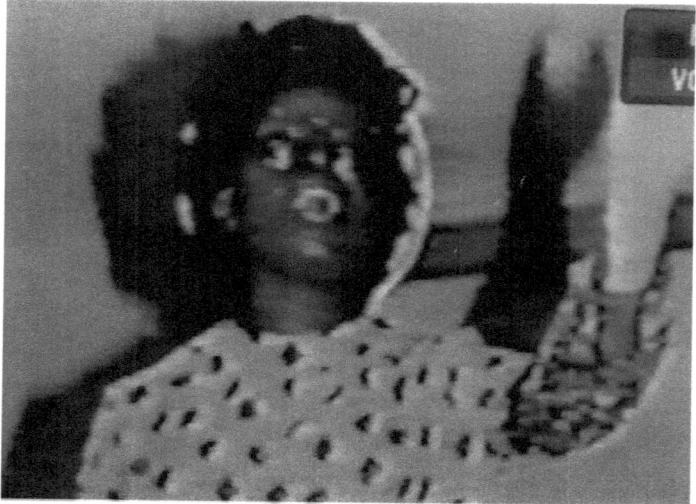

She Graduated Early: from Earth to Glory

one of their Dad-daughter excursions, they visited the Sweet Auburn Festival, which had an amateur stage for those who'd like to sing, and she volunteered to sing. Her doting father said the crowd was amazed, commenting about her BLESSED singing voice. Although she was beginning now to really become interested in boys, by now one in particular, she was still a Daddy's Girl as I'm sure you're beginning to notice.

During the wig-wearing days, she'd often leave it behind when she and he were out and about, don one of her special caps, and off they would go on their Saturday excursions and "I want" trips to the mall. Sometime, one of her friends, Haneefah or Tan, would join them. She'd often be interrupted by his desire to go to the flea market or thrift store to look at TVs to tinker on. She didn't like that part and would rush him on. After getting whatever outfit she desired, she'd say, "Dee Dee, get Mama a Double Doozie. She likes those." She'd get outfits and I'd get cookies. What's up with that? One time they even purchased a car. When Aubrey saw the first one he considered, she said, "No, Dee Dee, Mama won't like that one." Later, she saw another, a sporty one, and said, "Get this one, Dee Dee. She'll like this one." And I did. It grew on me! The problem was, I was hoping to enjoy NO CAR NOTE for a while after just finishing one. Duh!!!

Tee did not like missing school. Periodically, she'd have a fever, and whenever that happened, she'd have to be admitted to the hospital to be sure nothing serious (i.e. infection) was happening. Several times, she'd ask if she could be excused for a few hours, since the fever would have abated, as she'd want to go to a debate, or, once, an interview. When she was chosen as a North Georgia's McDonald's Black History Makers of Tomorrow, she, once again, had to "put on her game face," because they had to do a video with the winners. She looked soo good, soo healthy as she viewed the Georgia Capitol with such an expression of awe on her face. Sometimes the hospital staff did not know what to do with her but to say yes to her requests, if at a point that was medically safe for her. Because of the fever possibilities, sometimes her Dad would rub her head or grab her cheeks and she'd say,

"Dee Dee, I know what you're doing. You're trying to see if I have a fever." Of course, he'd deny it and often both were right. Sometimes doctor's visits were very unwelcomed because of what was to happen. Some would be spinal-tap visits so that they could check her bone marrow to see if she was leukemia-free. They'd have to insert the needle in the base of the spine and draw marrow. Tee'd just say, "Hold my hand, Mama/DeeDee." What a soldier she was!!!

Chapter 5

A Major Blessing on the Way

But now, back to the more JOYOUS times of her life. She was an award-winning debater, yearbook staff member, almost perfect "A" student, member of all honor societies (NFL, Beta, National Honor Society, Mu Alpha Theta—did I miss one?), cheerleader, chosen for her artistic talent for her July Calendar entry for C.U.R.E.'s annual calendar contest, and celebrated her Off-Chemo and Sweet Sixteen Party at the same time. Showered with love from friends and family. How AMAZING!!!!!!!!!

Now, though, amid so many good times, other serious decisions soon became necessary, as the doctors began to suggest that a bone marrow transplant might be necessary to insure stability, that the leukemia not return. Now off to testing family members to see if someone would be a match.

One day as I walked into her hospital room, during one of those "bumps in the road," she chuckled as she asked, "Guess who is a match?"

"Who?" I asked, excited that anyone matched.

She said, "Kirk!" and laughed that hearty laugh of hers when really tickled. Kirk, the younger of her older brothers, was, in his early childhood, afraid of his shadow at times. Kirk who, even though afraid, would do anything to help his baby sister. I recall the AWE with which he watched her when we brought her home from the hospital after her birth, like she was a very fragile AWESOME flower. This is the same Kirk whom I remember excitedly looking forward to meeting Pluto at Disney World, but when that moment came—and later the moment of meeting someone in an astronaut's outfit at Cape Canaveral—he literally shook in his boots. But this was her best friend and confidant, and one who'd bless her life to come. They'd often sit at the dinner table and solve all of the world's problems, or do the same as they walked the tracks at Therrell High School during the summer as their fitness efforts. Kirk was the brother who, two and a half years older than she, would be protected by her from the neighborhood bullies who teased him sometimes because he was so mild mannered. She'd threaten to run home and tell Dee Dee.

And so off now to the procedure and about two months in the hospital and at home. She could not wait to get back to school. Again, her homebound teacher came and assignments were taped, especially lectures by her teachers. Messages from students were sent. Prayers by many were lifted. Because Tee had been interviewed and passed the first level of approval for Governor's Honors, she was now concerned about the possibility of missing the final interview. She asked her nurses and doctor if she could be permitted to leave the hospital to go for her final interview, and they gave her the okay to do so. Often when such opportunities arose, we'd wonder how she really felt, but she'd put on her "game face/show-time face" and be off to do her very best, seemingly remembering her favorite Biblical promise: "I can do all things through Christ who strengthens me." Off she went with her father in tow, wishing her well. Needless to say, she passed the interview with flying colors!!!!! When she'd finished, she and her interviewer continued an extended conversation about some things they had in common. Dee Dee was amazed!

Chapter 6

God's Grace Magnified!

With healthy marrow and no need now to have the tube implanted in her chest to administer meds, they agreed with us that she could have it removed. Praise God!!!

During her 11th grade year, back at school without much interruption, chosen "Miss Junior," and recognized by our church, Ben Hill UMC, as a Young Woman of Distinction—all was well. Better still AWESOME!!! Tee was accepted to the ENDI (Emory National Debate Institute) for the second year, but this year she'd only attend for the first week, as Governor's Honors would begin the second week of the ENDI, and she'd prepare to go to Valdosta State College for the six-week program. From her first ENDI interview, she was quoted in a major ENDI promotion, which spoke to the importance of realizing and embracing the idea that people across all ethnicities have more commonalities than differences.

But now, another story. Excited though she was, when we prepared to say our good-byes as we left her at Valdosta State College for the Governor's Honors

Program, Tee began to boo-hoo like she'd never done before, not even during most of the treatments, EXCEPT when we took her older brother, Eric, to FAM-U for college. Then, too, when we prepared to say our good-byes to him, she just boo-hooed about leaving her  brother. But this time, this older Tee said, "You all are leaving me down here, and I don't know anyone." Well, we all had to talk fast, assuring her that she'd have a ball, meet many new people, and that, until she got adjusted, she could call home daily, and that her boyfriend (Edward) could even call her on our line, collect. Needless to say, although she soon became adjusted, she'd still call home each day just to see what we were doing and tell us what fun she was having. She did come home during July 4th holiday time for a doctor's checkup (and to see Edward) while home. Were we glad to see her!!! The other end of the story though is when we returned to bring her home at the end of the program, the boo-hooing began again. To this I said, "Oh no, don't you dare start," and we laughed as she spoke of the friends she'd miss and didn't want to leave. Go figure!

Her senior year was full of activity, full of hope. Tee's body seemed stronger than ever, which allowed her more cheering, more debating, and more honors, including being Second Attendant to Miss Harper High, on a clear track to becoming valedictorian of her class. But between the coronation and the declaration that she'd be valedictorian came another letdown/deflating of her/our balloon.

Near Thanksgiving, it was so ironic that she'd be told that the leukemia had returned and in a more aggressive form, not easily treated. We were all so devastated, and after she had her cry, her next remark was, "But we aren't going to give up and not do something, are we?" To that, her doctors decided to try one last treatment, and so off to school as usual, and with the hope that "This too shall pass" rekindled, we all went. In spite of it all, she continued to hold on to her claim of becoming valedictorian and gaining admission to college as she submitted applications.

Suddenly, seemingly out of the blue in April, she had a sharp pain in her side/abdomen area, and so off to the hospital we went, again. By this time, the valedictorian

She Graduated Early: from Earth to Glory

title was securely hers, as school would end in about a month. She would have days that she'd be at home, still with a teacher, but the last several weeks or so she was hospitalized. We'd share news with her of scholarships, schools that had accepted her, and still, for some reason, we did not accept death until it was  done, at least not really. We knew of the possibilities, but we knew whose final decision would determine the when. We were told that she now had contracted an infection that would steal our hope, that within a few days she'd pass. But even in spite of this, she again seemed to rebound, and after a week or so, though she seemed at peace with the possibility, I think her dad and I still held out hope. I never will forget her question to me one of the last days that she spoke. "What's taking so long?" She wasn't as worried about the *what* as she was about the length of time it was taking. I guess I had to hear that, yet I continued to hope. She and I held hands most of the day that would be her last, and when her dad came, she played with the hat on his head, turning it around like a rapper or young person, giving him a smile.

Chapter 7

GRADUATION TO HEAVEN

This is not meant to be a sad story but one from me to young people especially, but also to anyone who needs to be encouraged to live life to its fullest, no matter what the challenge. NO MATTER WHAT!!! On one of those last days on this side of Glory, as I relayed messages to Tee from others, she tried to say something that sounded like, "Go forward!" I asked if that is what she was saying, and she moved her head in affirmation.

GO FORWARD!!!!!!!!!!

I believe that God honors those who trust and have faith in Him, and finds ways to reveal that honor to them in return. I remember an afternoon during Tee's middle-school experiences, as she was returning from the funeral of a young lady who'd been hit by a bus, she asked me why some beautiful people die young, while some who are bad do not. I told her that I didn't know the answer, but I believed there are beautiful people who needed less time to get it right than did others. I asked if that made sense, to which she said, "Yes." As I think about her Youth Pastor, Rev Byron Thomas' comment, saying Tee's spirit outgrew her body, I would like to think that the two comments are relevant to her. He made reference to her sensitivity to the feelings of others, as she spoke to him once too of her desire to sing in the choir but her concern for how others might feel uncomfortable, those who knew her story. Rev. (soon to become Bishop) C. L. Henderson even opened the doors of the church during her celebration, and some fifty-plus youths came forth to give their lives to Christ that day. Tee's friend Haneefah, who gave remarks at her homegoing, closed her remarks with her decision to become a Christian on June sixth. Following her, Tee's Principal, Mr. Bibbs, encouraged students to seek spiritual connections so that their lives would be guided in the same direction as Tee's. A third remark from Rev. Henderson at the end of the Eulogy, a third confirmation of God's presence in this celebration, spoke to the importance of having a relationship with Christ as he opened the doors of the church, and (I only realized the impact as I watched the video again last week – twenty-four years later). I KNOW THAT MADE HER DAY!!!!

Another way that I think God honored Tee's faith in Him is the mysterious way that her story made

She Graduated Early: from Earth to Glory

coverage on three networks and radio stations and even in newspapers in South Georgia. I remember Steen Myles, then News Reporter for Channel 11, telling me that there is so much negative news that she "went to bat" with her producers to be given permission to cover Tee's AMAZING story. When we got home from the hospital that morning of her homegoing, someone called to ask if we were listening to the radio and directed us to do so. There was Tee's story. It was baffling to us. "What's going on?" we asked as it continued on and on and on throughout the week, with interviews at school and with us.

One of Tee's teachers called to share a story with us. She reminded me that it was raining that morning, even as that class period began, and she spoke of how heartbroken the students were. Some were crying but others, who were of strong faith as well, comforted the others, and they began to share Tee stories. Soon, during their sharing and laughing, they had not noticed that the rain had subsided and the sun had begun to shine. To them, that was a positive sign of her well-being, and God's presence in the midst of it all. Remember that I shared Tee's Governor's Honors experience with you. One of the students she'd miss, named Melanie, was from Buford, Georgia, and she and Tee kept in touch. For her birthday, she even invited Tee, who was in the hospital at that time, to attend her celebration at the Spaghetti Factory, and because it was near the end of one of those fever-related visits, she was permitted to go. On their way to Tee's homegoing celebration, her mom said that they were sooo quiet, but on the way home, they were full of chatter about Tee, her celebration, and other teen stuff, wanting to know if it was all right to laugh and feel the way they did, happy and at peace.

GOD would give me further PEACE, too. As we were on our way to her earthly burial site, I noticed that we were near our school and thought it would be nice if Rev. Henderson directed them to go that route. No sooner said that I noticed a turn in that direction. He also had the procession to stop in front of the school and he went to the back of the hearse, opened the door, and allowed Tee's spirit to say farewell to the place she'd loved so much. Tee smiled at this AMAZING Pastor

I'm sure. Listen to the song "One Moment in Time" after you've read Tee's story, and you cannot help but agree that that song is God's prophetic promise to Tee in return for her praise of Him, her commitment to being the kind of young lady who was determined to represent Him in all her ways, and in her encouragement to others to do and be likewise. HOW AWESOME IS THAT?

Chapter 8

BLESSED ASSURANCE

Now from GOD to me, another gift. A week or two later, I visited Tee's gravesite to share with her an award that she'd won. As I entered, I was playing gospel music, which I turned down in respect for the cemetery and those whose mortal beings rested there. After visiting with her, I returned to the car, and as I exited the cemetery, I turned the radio up only to hear, "Hello, Mother, I'm alright now. "I made it over and I'm alright now" and as the words continued, this song continued to bring me such PEACE as it spoke to my spirit. I'd never heard this song before, so you can imagine my reaction. After regaining my wits, I started looking for pen and paper to write the words down. The logical me led me to find out if this was a totally spiritual experience or was there really such a song. I found out that it was a real song, BUT, GOD, for me, for that moment. GLORY TO GOD!!!!!! THANK YOU, FATHER!!!!!

Because I taught Advanced Placement English, I was required to attend summer sessions relevant to that responsibility. While there the summer following Tee's homegoing, I met a teacher with whom I began a conversation which led to his recognizing me as Tee's mom, and he shared comments that his students who'd met her wanted to share. He taught in another city in North Georgia, and this was several months following her death. But God would again honor her faith as a father does for his child who trusts him and milks life as a way of blessing her father, too.

The month before that blessing, was graduation and another blessing afforded me to encourage Tee's classmates during what would have been her valedictorian moment to speak in the slot reserved for the valedictorian's message. I tried to express the many thoughts and concerns she'd want me to share with her classmates and others, even you. Tee would want you to remember: GO FORWARD!!!!!! NO MATTER WHAT THE CHALLENGES, THERE ARE ACCOMPLISHMENTS AND DESIRES THAT GOD WOULD HAVE YOU REALIZE. Even now as I think of her Youth Pastor, now Rev. Dr. Byron Thomas, who many years and a few appointments later, is now our Senior Pastor. Who would have believed we'd be blessed again with his presence? His wife, DuWanna, who was a friend/mentor to Tee, spoke of her memories of Tee in her first speech before the United Methodist Women, now as our SPECIAL First Lady.

REMEMBER ALWAYS: "**I can do ALL things** (that are meant to be YOURS TO DO, TO BECOME) **through CHRIST WHO STRENGHTENS ME**"!!! **GO FORWARD!!! BELIEVING!!!! HONORING!!!! LIVING LIFE TO YOUR FULLEST!!!** Tee would have you know that what God made possible for her, He'll make your moments available to you, too. One way that God BLESSED/HONORED Tee's life was done by making MOMENTS AVAILABLE to others for more than six years through **Emory Alumna Lillian Correa and Robinson-Humphrey**, who, through a grant, made it possible for the Barkley Forum to award a scholarship to a student, chosen each year as one who represented the values cherished by the Barkley Forum and represented in Tee's dedication to hard work, respect for others and excellence in academic performance. **God has BLESSED us, too** so that we could BLESS a college student each year for more than twenty years with a $500.00 Book Scholarship for their FAITHFULNESS to **those same values identified above, despite some challenge(s) which they could identify and were determined to overcome. LOOK FOR/ EXPECT…. BLESS HIM. TRUST HIM TO BLESS YOUR EFFORTS.** He's given you the talent, potential, and gifts to do MANY THINGS. **GO FORWARD, IN THE PRECIOUS NAME OF JESUS!!!**

An addendum to her story is an allegory written by Tee for her English class. It is my prayer that it, too, will bless you tremendously!

G C Attack
by Tazanya deAnn Maddox

CHARACTERS:

Leukemia
G C (God's Child)
Faith
Spirit

Setting: An apartment building in the Bay City area and the Bay City Amusement Park

G C: Oh, I'm so merry and happy today, for nothing harmful has come my way. My mind is free from trials and worry and is filled with thoughts so sweet and lovely. (There is a knock at the door.)

Leukemia: Hello, my name is Leukemia, and I want to be your friend. Come with me to the park to ride the rides, and then we will see which one you choose—Fear or Strength—and which video games you will lose.

G C: OK, I'LL GO WITH YOU TONIGHT. The house is clean and my schedule's light. What strange names to have for games, but I guess it's more exciting not to have the same ol' thing. (They leave for the amusement park.) The line for the ride called Fear is very long. Let's see what it is about. Come along. (They finally get to the gate to the ride.) Now, Leukemia, I hope you aren't afraid of this.

Leukemia: Afraid? No! Disease and I would hardly miss the ride. It's the first on our list. It is because of Fear that we came. It is scary to many but exciting to some. (They get on the ride.)

G C: We almost hit Death, Exams, and Pressure from Peers! There are many obstacles and special effects on this ride called Fear. (They exit.) Let's see what we can ride next. OOH, let's go do what I do best. (They go to the arcade.) I've never heard of this game before. I wonder why it's called Death, and why are the villains' names Illness, Sins, and Wealth? I understand the procedure now. I am to avoid the villains the best way I know how. (G C gets a top score.) Wow! Leukemia, I never would have learned to play this game had you not brought me here. Why don't we ride this ride, Strength, over there?

Leukemia: Well, I hate that ride. It's no fun to do. Look, there is Faith. He'll ride it with you. Faith!

Faith: Whatever could you want me for? We have not spoken since I turned you down when you approached my door. I see you have finally found a friend. Well, it won't be long before this friendship ends. I am true and you are not. You only arouse Fear and you have no heart.

G C: Why, Leukemia, is all of this true? I thought I could really trust you.

Leukemia: Well, that is what you get for thinking. Trust me when I say that this ride called Strength is boring. There is no line today or any day.

Faith: Ride it with me and you'll be fine. Anyone with a mind will determine to ride the ride by anything but the length of the line. (Faith and G C get into a cart.) Here we go. (Music plays.)

G C: The music in here is awesome, Faith. Fear has no music, no anything to make the ride great.

Faith: Some of the things you see are only illusions. They aren't really there. They only add to the amusement. Ride by Faith, not by sight. I will serve as a guide. I will explain all I know so this ride will, as smoothly as it may, go.

G C: Why do we go through this storm?

Faith: So that you may witness the situation's return to norm.

G C: Why do we move so slowly?

Faith: Because I have to answer your questions as we go. (They finish the ride after a series of questions and pleasant surprises.) That was not all bad, was it G C?

G C: Oh no. It was very nice to me. I gained much knowledge riding with you, and I came to know Strength and Leukemia, too.

Faith: Anytime you need a companion, call on me. My number is **LOV-EGOD**. I am available to ride any ride including the terrifying Fear. Actually, it is because of Fear also that I am here. It's better to ride with me than the disease Leukemia. That way you can enjoy and ride with ease.

G C: Thank you!

Spirit: So you see who remained when bad was near and far. Faith was willing to be a friend, so true, today and tomorrow. It was because of him that G C understood why the Creator sent (**allowed**) the fire and the flood on the attraction called Strength. He realized that he could beat Death, have Strength, and never be afraid (Fear) of the obstacles of every day.

THE END?...NOOO!
THE BEGINNING!!!
God has not given us a spirit of fear; but of power, and of love, and of a sound mind.
2 Tim. 1:7

Awards/Recognitions/Achievements (through Christ who strengthened her)

- Member of Ben Hill United Methodist Church, where she served faithfully through the Cherubs, Children's, and Youth choirs, and through Sunday School—from two years old through her senior year in high school.
- Young Ladies of Distinction recognition at Ben Hill UMC
- Tested/Accepted into the Challenge/Gifted Program from Preschool throughout High School (Honors and Advanced Placement Student in HS)
- School choruses throughout MS and HS (also inspirational soloist for banquets, funerals, and other programs)
- Cheerleader for community centers' athletic programs through elementary school and a Bunche Middle School/Harper High School Varsity cheerleader
- Major roles in two middle school musicals
- Participant/winner Ford Motor Company Family Talent Show, Ben Hill UMC Talent Show
- Language Arts Award for the Most Authentic-Sounding Spanish Solo
- Recipient of MANY debate and speech awards
- Participant in a Sweet Auburn Festival Public Mike Activity

- Student Body and Church Leadership (children/youth)
- Service through C.U.R.E. (volunteer: cancer and leukemia support groups for children)
- July Calendar Winner (C.U.R.E. art work competition)
- Member: Mu Alpha Theta Math Honor Society, Beta Honor Society, National Honor Society, NFL Forensics Honor Society
- North Georgia Winner: McDonald's Black History Makers of Tomorrow
- Member: Who's Who Among America's High School Students
- Valedictorian of Harper High School's Class of 1993
- Academic Incentive Award Winner in Language Arts
- Miss Junior, 1991–1992
- Second Attendant to Miss Harper High, 1992–93
- Governor's Honors Winner/Participant—Valdosta State College (six-week summer program)
- College acceptances before homegoing: Morris Brown College, Clark-Atlanta University, Emory University, Judson, Fort Valley State University, Oglethorpe University
- Scholarship awards from AKA Sorority: Kappa Omega Chapter, Ben Hill United Methodist Church, Clark Atlanta University, Emory University, Oglethorpe University (with others still pending)

IN GRATITUDE FOR PRAYERS, LOVE, CARE, SUPPORT, AND FRIENDSHIP THROUGH IT ALL

- Mrs. Susie H. Jessie, her Grandmother/caregiver
- Mrs. Annie J. Goss, her Aunt/caregiver
- Other family members
- Rev. Dr. Byron Eric Thomas, her supportive Youth Pastor
- Mrs. DuWanna Thomas, Wife to Rev. Thomas/supportive friend/mentor
- Bishop Cornelius Henderson, Former Pastor for many years/Eulogist
- Rev. Leon Matthews, Care Ministry at Ben Hill UMC
- Rev. McCallister Hollins, our then recently appointed Pastor who supported our family in many related ways
- Rev. JunAnn Johnson, family friend/supportive care, and prayer warrior
- Mrs. Lois Toney, family friend/supportive care
- Mrs. Iona Walker, family friend, prayer warrior
- Ben Hill UMC Bible Study and Prayer Ministry
- Mrs. Sydney, special encourager at Egleston Children's Hospital
- Nurse C. J., Tee's special IV nurse/supportive friend at Egleston

- Nurse Salley, special nurse/support at Egleston
- Mrs. Nan, special nurse/support at Egleston
- Dr. Alvarado, Tee's main doctor at Egleston
- Dr. Kim, other medical support staff at Egleston
- Mrs. Bessie Monroe, Homebound Teacher
- Mrs. Melissa M. Wade and other Emory/Barkley Forum Family who awarded her two+ ENDI scholarships, nurtured her and assisted in perfecting her debate skills and,
- **Emory Alumna Lillian Correa and Robinson-Humphrey**, a grantor who made it possible for the Barkley Forum to award an ENDI scholarship to a student each year for more than six years.
- Ben Hill United Methodist Church's 1993 Youth Choir for dedicating its concert that year to Rev. Byron E. Thomas, **then**, Youth Minister; NOW, Rev. Dr. Byron Eric Thomas, Sr. Pastor of Ben Hill UMC **AND** in Memory of Tazanya
- ALL of Tazanya's (TEE'S) TEACHERS, who provided written, video, and audiotaped notes/homework, while out for hospital stays
- SPECIAL C. L. HARPER HIGH SCHOOL FRIENDS/FAMILY
- FRIENDS AND EMPLOYEES OF FORD MOTOR COMPANY
- OUR SPECIAL BEN HILL UMC FAMILY FOR MANY PRAYERS, OTHER ACTS OF LOVE AND SUPPORT
- **Eric M. Maddox, her big brother and the artist who lovingly designed the book cover portrait of her**

www.ingramcontent.com/pod-product-compliance
Lightning Source LLC
Chambersburg PA
CBHW061805070526
44586CB00023B/2722